From Bullets to the Ballot

Uncovering the Political Truth About the African American Vote

By Tony Herbert

ISBN-13: 978-0-578-75475-8

Publisher's Note

Dedication

I dedicate this book to my mother, Ms. Yvonne Theresa Herbert. My guardian angel who is and always has been my inspiration to strive to do my very best with what I have, while always being a help to others along the way. Thank you for never giving up on us. I love you mom and miss you every single day.

I dedicate this book to my kids, Brittany, Anthony Jr., Antone, Mehki and Aaliyah. You all are an inspiration to me to go further than I have ever imagined and not a day goes by that I am not gleaming and declaring how proud I am of you all! Thank you for allowing me to be your dad!

I dedicate this book to my mentor, my confidant and adopted god father, Mr. Cliff Lever. Thank you Pops for being there for me and giving me the tools needed to be the man I am today. I know you are in heaven looking over me and telling my mom about all the crazy times we had. Your presence is felt every day in the work I do and I really and truly appreciate you for helping to get my life jumpstarted.

I especially want to dedicate my book and thank my wife, Leah, for all her support and encouragement. Thank you, babe!

Lastly, I dedicate this book to My Lord and Savior Jesus Christ. Thank You for your mercies, many blessings and patience with me as I get my Christian faith together! Thank you Lord!

Foreword

From Bullets to Ballot is the story of Tony Herbert's astounding journey. Growing from a youth, raised in a single parent household-often living in dangerous situations-to a man whose life lessons taught by his loving mother, drives him to help others.

His fight to improve conditions for people living inside New York City Public Housing Projects has placed him in a position where he is called upon to serve in many capacities. Whether he is liaising with Police brass, or marching on New York City Hall to stop the gun violence, Tony Herbert is a man of action-always working to improve the lives of New Yorkers while calling out neglect and corruption. It's no wonder that leaders of both major political parties have sought Tony out to run for office. This book makes the reader wonder what the next chapter of his life will bring.

Leticia Remauro, President and CEO

The Von Agency Public Relations

From Bullets to the Ballot

Contents

Prologue

If someone would have told the younger version of me that one day I'd be indirectly involved with the shooting of a politician, I wouldn't have believed them. I would have bet all the money I had on me at the time, which probably would not have been much. But I would have made the bet and lost.

Now, I'm not the shit-starter type of guy, so just the thought of someone thinking I shot someone was insane. I'm a peaceful guy. I like bringing my people together. You know, throw on some music, have a good time. In fact, that's what I did for many years. And then I called myself trying to be the standup guy and fight for my people.

Back when I was a young guy, I had a mentor who put me up on the game of politics. I found it interesting enough to pursue an opportunity to work on a political campaign when an opportunity presented itself. Working on a campaign led to me actually running a campaign – for myself.

What started out as something genuine, turned ugly.

In August 2003, I got caught up in a huge political scandal that impacted my journey to becoming an activist in my community. I called myself trying to prove somebody wrong and found myself running for the City Council. What a mess it turned out to be! I had no clue what I was getting myself into.

One day, I'm preparing to beat the current occupant in a race for his seat, and the next, I'm being surrounded by cops who think that I may or may have not killed Councilman James E. Davis.

From Bullets to the Ballot doesn't just chronicle my journey of becoming the man that I am today. It gives a backstage view of what it's like to be on the front line as a community leader and it's my way to share the importance of voting. This book gives you insight on what really goes down on a campaign trail, and the true reason why all people of color should vote. While you'll be entertained, you'll be even more informed of what politics are really like, why it's important to get to know your political leaders and most importantly – *to vote.*

Chapter One

How Did I Get Here?

You have a different perspective on life when your mom is a struggling single parent, living in a tenement and your father lived around the corner from you in a Brownstone with a pool in the backyard with his wife and your half brothers and sisters. Your thought process and level of compassion is slightly different than the average person. You travel down a different path to get to the same destination as the thought-leaders and visionaries in this time. Nevertheless, you get there. But because of the life you started out with, sometimes you have to pause and ask yourself: *how did I get here?*

I'd love to say I got here because my father introduced me to so and so that opened up opportunities such as this. Or that my mom was a millionaire who put me in the finest of schools to get such and such degree. But that's not how I got here.

Somedays, I think I got here because of my wit. Other days, I think I got here because of my intelligence. Most days, I remember I got here because I grew up with a single mother raising four boys on her own around the corner from their father who was married to someone else. So, he denied them. Publicly and emotionally.

I mean, I guess I understand why he would deny my brothers and I in court. After all, he had a wife and family. A wife that was not my mother. I get it. But it was still wrong. It wasn't my fault that my father had two families that lived around the corner from each other. But we suffered from his choices. I wasn't able to experience the day-to-day interactions with my father because, well, he chose not to.

My mom, on the other hand, took pride in raising us. Although she raised us by herself, she made it look easy. Not only did she take pride in her parenting skills, but she also took pride in her work. She worked in the local public-school system and did a lot of the grunt work as a school aide. And even though she didn't make a lot of money, she did what most black single mothers do: she made it work.

Like most single-parent households in Brooklyn, we were living paycheck-to-paycheck. My mom brought home a salary of next to nothing. We didn't get all the luxuries we wanted to have. It was pretty bad. At one point, I had to share pants with my brothers. But my mom did the best she could raising four boys by herself. While my grandmother was around in my earlier years, it wasn't her responsibility. It was my father's. But he was too busy tending to his other family around the corner and pretending as if the four kids he had by mother didn't exist. We were evidently a secret. A secret that wouldn't stay between just the adults anymore.

The Family Tree

While I knew something wasn't right about my father not living with us, I didn't dig too much. I was young. I had no understanding of the issues between the two families my father created. At some point, I became accustomed to not seeing my father regularly, although he came by to see my mom for some physical attention here and there. Once I realized he wasn't trying to make an effort to get to know me or us, I let it go. After finding out I had siblings from his marriage, my father wasn't the one I was interested in getting to know any longer. I wanted a relationship with my brothers and sisters, so I found myself trying to make time to get to know them and build on our kinship.

Doing so was a bit of a challenge because they had been told that we weren't related. At one time, we all lived on Prospect Place, and then when I was about eight years old, we moved around the corner to Park

Place. My half-brother Chris and I wound up in the same class in the sixth grade.

When my mom found out who I was now hanging out with, she told me that he was my brother on my father's side. I recall my mom having a picture of our dad in our home, so I took it and I showed it to him, feeling vindicated because of his denial, but hoping he would accept that we were brothers.

We started hanging out with each other by Pinkie Pie, playing stickball block against block, and that was when it started really getting into the heavy conversations about us being related.

I told my biological brothers that I wanted us to get to know our half-brothers and sisters. Boy did that cause a little friction. They would ostracize me because they felt that I was trying to be better than them, and that was so far from the truth. I just wanted to have a relationship with them because they were doing exciting things and having fun doing it.

My half-sister, who is the oldest, was the one that helped to cement our relationship. She was the one who told my father and stepmother, "I'm going to have a relationship with them. Those are our brothers and you know they are."

My father admitting we were his children wasn't easy or something that happened overnight. Actually, he told them that my oldest brother, Brian, was his only child with my mom. Implying my mom was some thot out there getting knocked up by other dudes. That pissed me the hell off when I heard it. Him finally admitting the truth had a lot to do with my Grandma Emma.

The Truth Is Uncomfortable

My mother's mother was straight up gangsta and not one to play with out of Northeast Washington, DC. She was truly a sweet woman, but when she started drinking and cussing, people got out her way. One particular occasion, my grandmother got fed up with our dad denying us and she made her way around the corner to his home. My mother's mother went to confront my father and his mother (Nanna Myrtis) and told my father's mother, "I will whoop you and your son's ass if you he doesn't get out here and take care of his responsibility."

It's a strong and confident woman who'll march onto someone else's porch giving demands. That's the type of woman my grandma Emma was. My father's mother on the other hand, was very, very bourgeois. She had that *I've arrived* kind of personality, but she was no joke either, rest her soul. For whatever reason, she did not encourage my father to acknowledge us, let alone support us or at least that was what I assumed. Whatever my paternal grandmother's reasons were for not encouraging our father to interact with us, my maternal grandmother wasn't trying to hear that. In her mind, he had a responsibility she wanted him to take care of and he wasn't doing that, so she had no problem going over there and calling him out.

Unfortunately, seeing my grandmother bad mouthing my absent father was normal. It may have been awkward to hear, but well, it was the truth. My father lived minutes away from me and my siblings, yet none of us had a relationship with him. He acted as though we were just kids from around the corner that played with his children that his wife birthed. When the reality was that my brothers and I were conceived and birthed around the same time my half-siblings were conceived and birthed. One of my half-brothers and I are a week apart. How's that for a reality check?

But I wasn't allowed in that house. And the only reason I wasn't allowed was because of what was apparently happening between my father, Grandma Emma, and his mother, Nanna.

I was about fourteen years old when I experienced being told I couldn't come inside their home. We were all hanging out in the Terminals down in the Fort Greene section of Brooklyn on this one particular day. It was a hot, sweaty day. My half-brother Keith said, "You know what? It's hot! Let's all go get in the pool."

I got a little excited because I'm thinking, *Yes! I'm in there.* Here we all are, going back to this house to get in the pool. The pool I've watched from my backyard time and time again. No way that they would be so mean as to tell me that I couldn't come in because there were other kids here, and some of them were practically strangers. When we got to the house, unsurprisingly I was told to wait a second. Chris and Keith said they had to get permission for me to come in. I was a little thrown off, but I tried not to let it show.

I stood at the gate in anticipation, waiting for one of them to come back to get me. I was beginning to get a little anxious, since I could hear the other kids in the back having fun and I wanted to have fun as well. Finally, Keith came back to the gate. He said, "We're asking Nanna could you come in now because Dad is acting like a fool."

I continued to wait. They again asked Nanna and then they asked their mother. When it was all said and done, after waiting there about forty-five minutes for somebody to give me a positive response, my Nanna came to the door. She told me, "I'm not going to allow the boys to have any more company. Everybody's getting ready to go home because I want to get me some sleep."

Damn! I remember walking away with my head down and this deep, hurtful feeling that felt like someone just sucker punched me in my soul.

The lesson learned from that experience taught me that I would never follow behind anybody ever again, trying to be accepted. In addition, I'd never put myself in the position to hear the word *no* ever again!

Eventually, I stopped putting in the effort to get to know my father and half-siblings. I embarrassed myself to a large degree trying to build that relationship, but I took the chance because I realized that I really wanted to have a relationship with them.

I don't remember when the turning point was, but at some point, I was allowed to enter the house. It took me a while to be comfortable around them. I was still on eggshells because I needed to understand the circumstances. I never told my mother that they turned me away from that door. She would've been livid, and I didn't want her to go over there and cuss anyone out.

For a while, I wasn't quite sure how to feel or what to think about my reality. I didn't understand why my mom would have multiple kids by my father.

He clearly didn't want to be bothered with us. The man lived close enough to build a relationship. Everyone already knew my father had two families, so what was the issue with him reaching out to us? Why didn't my mom try and make him do so, like my grandmother did? I just didn't understand. So, I asked mom why she had four kids by someone who didn't respect her enough to help her out, since she didn't make us all by herself. She said, "Well, you know that's what love will do to you. Make you blind and stupid at times." And that's how it was explained to me, so I didn't ask about it anymore. My father got a pass for not being a father because my mother was in love with that fool.

My truth: my father had two families and only supported one. The one that I wasn't a part of. And it really affected me growing up.

My Mentor Saved My Life

I had to do an extra six months of high school because I was so stressed out that I had no male influences in my life. I responded by cutting class, cutting school and failed my main shop class that I had to repeat. I was playing with guns and picking fights to earn a reputation in school, when I knew my ass wasn't built for a real fight at that time. The little martial arts classes I took just wouldn't be enough to deal with those big dudes. I was acting out and wanted to be a tough guy. I was acting on being told that, "If you want to be respected and not picked on, pick a fight with the biggest bully in the room/class. You may very well get your ass beat but you will earn some respect."

My mom basically had done all she could do to get us where we were. We needed a positive male role model available to teach us how to be men, but no one was around. At some point, my mom had to start her life again, and so she did. She started dating again. By doing that, she got involved in her own world and when that happened, I felt some kind of way. I thought, *my mom got a man now and she ain't got no time for me, but she's allowing me to stay out later.* As a teen, that was cool, but not what I needed. While I was able to hang out late, I had to acclimate myself to understanding what that responsibility meant. I was really on my own, but I didn't need to be. I needed some guidance. I needed to know what to do in life after I graduated high school. I was hanging out at the parties in the school yards and saw things that scared the crap out of me. I saw a guy get shot in his head and his brain matter splattered all on the ground. I witnessed a guy I grew up with get shot in a basement party I attended and had to step over him in order to get out. I remember looking back, thinking, *I should help him*, but the fear the shooters may come back and that the police might be on the way had me running for my life.

As life would have it, I met a mentor who shifted the trajectory of my life. Enter Leopold C. Lever, Mr. Cliff, or Cliff, as we would all affectionately call him. This man unselfishly introduced me to things in life that made me forget that I was growing up in a fatherless environment. Unfortunately, I wasn't the only young man who grew up in a single parent household. Hell, we all needed the structure he provided. Mr. Cliff gathered up all the young people in our community and created an atmosphere for us to get involved in positive activities. His commitment to us gave us a sense of belonging that shaped us all into who we are today.

Mr. Cliff, a Panamanian who became a citizen of the United States in the early sixties. He served in our military with honors and was involved with a club called the Crown Heights Lions Club. It was a chapter of Lions Clubs International, so we became members of that chapter's youth division, called the Crown Heights Leo club. We started getting exposed to business leaders, community activists and politicians and it was there that the seed of community outreach and politics was planted in my mind.

We were taught how to dress properly when going to meetings, how to conduct meetings. Mr. Cliff along with a few others that adopted us like Dyanne Norris, Campbell Rudder, Bernice McPherson, and Mister and Misses Henry Samuels, the senior elders who made sure that we had an understanding of the dynamics of community and politics and all of the stuff that goes into what it takes to be in the game of life. They all created an opportunity for us when we were in the Leos club to go to the Lion's Club's annual convention in 1983 held in Honolulu, Hawaii, and we were to speak before then President Ronald Reagan. Mr. Cliff and Mr. Samuels paid a portion of the travel fees for me, and my mom contributed what she could. So, I was on my way, for the first-time leaving New York on a plane, I was on my way to Hawaii! Chris and I both were a part of the delegation that went to represent our Leo Chapter along with a couple of others, like our then president Doriana and one of our board members Michelle.

Cliff truly positioned me in an atmosphere that screamed opportunity. I learned a lot about community and politics, in which I got a little deeper than I expected.

Having a mentor/father figure was truly life changing. He taught us a lot of different things and that was what helped to shape me and the guys in our neighborhood into the men we are today. Well, I know that to be true for myself personally. I was just getting into high school when this man came into my life and when I became of age, he let me use his car to learn how to drive. He even gave me the coat literally right off his back when I started wearing suits. He was kind enough to invite some of us into his house to meet and interact with his family. We became a part of his family. I mean literally we would go in his refrigerator and get something to eat. His wife Olivia, whom I call mom till today would cook on Sundays and we would eat dinner with them sometimes. If we didn't have any money or whatever, we could borrow between him and his wife. My mentor is the same man who got me my first job as I graduated out of high school and got me a job in the banking industry. This is the kind of influence that he brought us.

It was in October of 1980. I believe our chapter of the Leos club had just participated by marching in the Columbus Day parade. It was about six p.m. that evening when we were all still together hanging out on the block up the street from Mr. Cliff's house and I got a brain fart to have a foot race in the street against Keith who had bragged that he was the fastest amongst us and I felt the need to challenge that bravado. We jumped out in the middle of the street as did a few others who also wanted in on this race and the girls yelled go. We took off and need I say I felt I won however Keith would tell the story differently.

But what had happened at the end of the race at the finish line really took us by surprise and changed our lives forever. There were some auxiliary cops patrolling the community and they had summoned Keith to come over to them. By the time we could ask what's up, they had Keith in handcuffs. Both Chris and I went running over to ask what the hell was up and next thing we knew we were both in handcuffs.

Apparently, a middle eastern man was just robbed of his brief case and three dollars and he said Keith looked like the guy that robbed him. The auxiliary cops overreacted and figured they had an arrest. To add insult to injury the victim said that Chris and I were his accomplices. What? How the hell could we commit such a damn crime when we had a host of witnesses screaming at them that we had nothing to do with that? The fake cops panicked as the whole community was screaming on them and they called the real Police for backup and next thing I knew we were on our way in handcuffs to the Seventy-Eighth Precinct house. All my fears about jail became a reality for me, but how could this be when I just participated in something so positive earlier in the day? We just weren't those kids so what now? The jails were full at central booking so they transported us to the

Seventy-First Precinct to spend the night and said we would make court in the morning. Huh? My father came to the precinct and was ask by the detectives did he speak for us all and he hesitated when it came to me. I gave him such a look, like *now isn't the time for your bullshit, you better tell them I am your child!* With what seemed like reluctance he said yes, and all I could think in my mind was where is my Mom and Mr. Cliff? I was truly afraid of the unexpected.

Mr. Cliff did in fact come to the precinct as well and that gave me a sense of relief. He told me he would notify my Mom and not to worry because he had my back. We got released on our own recognizance and had a court date to return. What I witnessed was miniscule to what awaited us in that cell. Some guys beat a guy bad because he was in for robbing and assaulting an old lady. All I knew was that I wanted out of that place because I wouldn't survive, and all the stories of the homosexuality and gang rape of men committed just didn't sit well with me, no matter how much I could defend myself.

I was also very concerned for my brothers, albeit they kept Chris and I together. They always put Keith in a separate cell, and we couldn't help him if he got into anything.

My father and Nanna got us an attorney, well they got Keith and Chris an attorney and added me in because my story had to be the same as theirs. We returned to court sometime later and were told if we didn't get into any more trouble within six months that the case would be sealed, but if we did it would be reopened and used against us. *Wait! We didn't do a damn thing and we were being treated like this?* I didn't want a record or blemish because of this bull on my record. I had never been arrested or ticketed for anything and now this? I needed to get out of the city, it was too much to absorb!

Homelessness

One of my mother's brothers, Uncle Bobby, owned a house in Uniondale, Long Island. He and his wife, Joan, would invite my brothers and I to come out on weekends to spend time with them and our cousins. We alternated spending the weekend out there just to get away from Brooklyn for a while. Because my uncle had four daughters and no son, I know that he enjoyed it when me and my brothers came to visit. We also got a chance to interact with a father-figure, so it was always a good time. The time I spent in Long Island was usually positive and the escape I needed from the craziness. So, most of my memories are good. Well, except for one. I just happened to be there that weekend when I got a phone call telling me that we moved. And my question was, "We moved? To where?"

I knew that my mother didn't make a lot of money, so it worried me to learn that when I got back to Brooklyn, that I'd be living in a different place. I learned that we moved across the street. I also learned about gentrification because that was what happened to us. We were forced to move due to Brooklyn being in the beginning phases of gentrification. It was really weird. Gentrification clearly represented if you don't have the money, you must move. This was the only neighborhood that I knew so it was an uncomfortable truth. We only had three options since we couldn't afford to stay: we either had to live on the street, go to a shelter or rent another place.

My mom just didn't have it financially to move. At the time, her weekly take home net salary was around $200. We couldn't afford to move to another apartment. So, she moved us across the street into a huge, abandoned apartment building. Yep, we were now going to be Squatters. I know it wasn't easy for my mom to do this because it wasn't easy for me!

We lived across the hall from the drug dealers. Not ideal for a single mother with four boys, but she had to do what she felt was best at the time. She didn't worry about us going down that path because she didn't play. Even the drug dealers on my block didn't try my mother. They knew she wasn't afraid to speak her mind. But I recall them telling my mom she didn't have to worry about us getting involved in that criminal world, they would kick our ass and send us home if we tried. You see, most of them either attended or had kids that attended PS9. My mom knew her from there and respected her greatly because she was a mothering figure to them as well to a degree.

I don't know where the gas and lights came from in the apartment they chose for us to move into because that entire building was off the grid. I had to call somebody to let them know I was coming home, so somebody would meet me in the lobby with a flashlight. Often there was no running water or lights in the common areas for the building. We had to literally go outside to the fire hydrant also known as a water pump, to get a bucket or two of water to take back upstairs to use for bathing, drinking, and flushing the toilet. They had stolen the copper pipes out of the basement, so we had no running water. I mean nothing worked. We lived like this for eight and a half months.

Do you know today that very building is now a multimillion-dollar property with some of the most expensive coops /condos in that part of Brooklyn?

Good ole gentrification.

Fortunately, our homelessness didn't last for too long. Eventually I got a job thanks to Mr. Cliff. After eight months, I was able to save money, put it with some of my mother's money, and move into a building a couple of doors down that was more suitable for us to live in. You see Mr. Cliff put a word in for me at the bank just as I graduated from high school. He was a Manager at Bankers Trust down by the World Trade Center in Manhattan and got me hired as a long-term temp.

My mom lived there until she died in 1999. I finally moved out of that apartment in Prospect Heights in 2007.

Path to Politics
When you're in the midst of a problem, you rarely think about the positive side of the

ordeal. You just know that being in a bind sucks, and you want to get out of it. That was my mentality about homelessness. It sucked! And I did everything that I could to try to get out of it. I had no clue this experience would be what sparked my interest in getting involved with politics.

The experience of being homeless reminded me of something that I learned through the Lion's Club. Politicians were supposed to help you when you have issues and our living arrangements facing homelessness was an issue. So, I went to a senator for guidance. I told then State Senator Velmanette Montgomery, who was the senator for our community about my family's homeless situation and her response disappointed me. Here I am thinking my local politicians would have my back, but I learned otherwise. Rather than give me resources or guidance to prevent becoming homeless, I was told to go into a shelter and that there's nothing she can really do. That pissed me off. My thing was you got elected by us to help us, so you should know something. Since I wasn't satisfied with her lack of knowledge, this made me want to step my game up and fill the void that I felt was missing.

Chapter Two

Learning the Game

Before I dove into the political game, I was fully invested in the nightlife. For a long while, I was an independent radio and video show producer, party promoter and soon elevated to become the marketing director for a nightclub. I never planned to work at a nightclub, but I got asked to come in to help the new owner of Club Elite formerly known as Club Savage in midtown Manhattan by my good friend Don Welch who happened to be the main DJ there. I was brought in to help fill the place out because they were losing business to some heavy competition from a white mobbed owned newly opened club called the Shadow. There were also other independent promoters chipping away at their attendees because they were booking ballrooms to host their parties. After successfully helping rejuvenate the attendance numbers, the owner for whatever reason wasn't paying the rent and wound up having the club shut down by the landlord. Damn all that hard work and folk just weren't professional, not paying your bills will get you shut down, hello!

Next thing you know I'm running for city councilman.

I'm often asked, "How did you go from working at a nightclub to working in politics?" Well, long story short, I was always the consummate networker, and after seeing the marshal's eviction notice on the door of the club, I had to think of something fast to make money asap. I now had three kids who needed to be provided for, my daughter Brittany, sons Anthony and Antone, and going back to the banking industry was the last thing on my mind but just may have been my last option if this entrepreneurial spirit didn't bare some fruit. So, I jumped out and did some ad sales work for the Big Black Book.

The BBB was a directory of sort, like a yellow pages for Black owned business. One day I found out that some business professionals were going to be at an event/fundraiser for a politico I knew back when I was a youth in the Leo Club and figured that was as good a place as any to seek some ad sales for the BBB. So, I invited a friend named Malika Moran/Founder of SocialStep.com who started the first ever professional network website here in New York to join me as I knew she always liked networking too. At the event, I met a brother named Darren Pearson who was heavy into real estate and figured I'd pitch him on buying an ad for his business. He invited me to come by his office the next day to discuss the book and the ad purchasing process. That's when I found out that he wasn't just some guy, he was the President of The Men's Caucus for Congressman Ed Towns.

Remember I stated that I knew this politician when I was a youngster in the Lion's Club? So, Darren and I chatted for a while about what I was doing, and all that the Congressmen's group was doing. Mind you, he never purchased the ad. But I did come out of the meeting with an offer that proved to be more valuable than the ad, as I was asked to chair the youth committee for The Men's Caucus in support of the Congressman. It was a no-brainer to work for him. And I'm glad that I did. I knew being affiliated with him would put me in rooms that afforded me some opportunities of a lifetime. One being that I would be asked to work for one of the most powerful elected female politicians in NYC who was very tight with then Mayor Giuliani.

It all started when the congressman asked if I would volunteer some weekends to help the Councilwoman campaign as she was running for re-election. I really didn't know at that time that I was going to be helping one of the most powerful Black women in the state of New York. I mean, I knew she was a big deal, but wasn't fully aware of just how big of a deal she truly was. I'd soon find out just how powerful this lady was.

Once I started working for her, I had access to some powerful people. I saw a lot and I heard a lot. More importantly, I learned a lot. Being able to study someone as politically astute as she was really paid off for me years later. In my mind, I didn't deserve a seat at such a dynamic table. Here I am, a young guy from Brooklyn, not accustomed to this whole political game, with nothing more than a high school diploma in rooms with some of the key decision-makers of New York City. I had a front-row seat to witness greatness in action and I loved it. As a young guy, I heard about people like her, but to see it up close and personal was amazing. The governor, the mayor, union officials and other heads of state would all come by her house on any given Sunday to taste her southern cooking. I was around the political elite, not sure what exactly was going on, but I was there. I just knew that it was official, and a lot of big things were being talked about, some I was privy to and most I often had to leave the room.

One thing I can say about Councilwoman Wooten is that she taught me a lot. I watched it all from the sidelines, all of the deceit, all of the crabs in a barrel activity she endured. I saw her having to fight twice as hard being a woman. They were being disrespectful to her. Although I didn't agree with how she was being treated, I didn't say anything. I just watched it because that's how I learned. To be honest, at one point it was stressing me out. Her schedule was so demanding. It had become totally difficult for me to keep up with. I barely had a life of my own. And that wasn't good. The relationship that I was in at the time failed because I didn't have time to commit to it. I was so busy working my ass off that I couldn't be a good boyfriend to the young lady I was seeing. When my relationship ended because of my position with the Councilwoman, I started to reassess my decision to stay on board. It had gotten so bad that I developed anxiety attacks.

I remember it like it was yesterday. She was invited to go to an event and needed me to drive her. I wasn't really feeling this event because one, it was two hours long and two, because the time wasn't good for me. See, at the time, I didn't have my car. My ex-wife took it in our divorce, so I had to catch several trains and a bus as that became my transportation norm to and from work. So, that meant that I needed to catch these damn things in -order to get home at a decent hour to spend time with her. Well, this two-and-a-half-hour event would have made me miss my train, so I didn't want to go. This caused a huge, and heated, debate between her and I. I didn't understand why it was a debate. She knew that I didn't have proper transportation. The time that the event was scheduled to end was after the trains would be accessible. I was so pissed that she decided to go and that caused my stress level to instantly spike.

Once the event was over, I rushed out of there to head home. Walking wasn't getting me away from that place fast enough, so I started running for the bus. I got on the bus and all of a sudden, I couldn't catch my breath. I tried to slow myself down, talk to myself mentally and what not. But that didn't work too well. My breathing was still choppy and hard to calm down. I transferred from the bus to the train. Because I was running to catch the train, I ignore the fact that I still couldn't breathe. After getting on the train, I realized that my not being able to breathe was getting worse. I needed some fresh air. But that wasn't going to happen anytime soon. The first stop was at least three-minutes from the next. It was within those three minutes that I realized what was going on. I was having a full-blown anxiety attack.

I realized that working for the Councilwoman was too stressful and I needed to find another profession. But what was I going to do?

However, I did resign and was able to secure a position with Congressman Towns. Oh boy, that was an adventure in itself, but damn I was now able to gain access to the Halls of Congress. Sadly not even a full month into working for the Congressman I got the news from my mom's doctor while sitting at my desk that she had a severe case of ovarian cancer and there was nothing that could be done to save her life. I hid my heartache knowing this from my mom and tried to put a smile on my face every time she and I would talk. But I saw my mom disappearing in front of me, my mom went from being this awesome gorgeous woman full of life with an awesome smile, figure and personality that made you feel good about yourself. She smiled when times were hard, and yet I would catch her holding back tears of stress over bills and putting food on the table. I would give anything to have her back right now and make her feel her worries are no longer of a concern, her son is successful and able to take care of her with no issue, I miss her so much. She passed away quickly on July 5th, 1999.

I worked with the Congressman for a little over a year and realized I wasn't happy because I reported directly to his district chief of staff, who was a known alcoholic and very disgusting. You could be standing there talking to her and she would literally reach behind her back to pull her pants or whatever the hell it was out of her ass. Ugh, disgusting! To top it off I felt she was an undercover racist. So, we bumped heads often until I had had enough. I did not come to work for a Black man to be disrespected by this nasty, racist, white woman. To add insult to injury, he had a district director that nobody cared for as she too had issues. I just thought she didn't believe her stuff stank and she thought she was better than everyone else, but her fat old ass was just as bad as the chief of staff.

Don't get me wrong, I had some good times working for the Congressman and he praised me for my work, but he also didn't do much to control some of the crazy things that these two were doing that forced a lot of staff to leave. The revolving door in most elected officials' offices is all the rave. Just know the pay isn't that great and they expect you to give up your whole life to help them live their life. So, I did what I thought was best. I resigned very dramatically by cussing her out as I walked out the door. Yep! I gave her an earful that I believe a lot of the staff was wanting to say as well.

Just before I resigned, I was contacted by the White House. Yep they called ya boy a few weeks before I resigned to help out with some upcoming campaigning. The First Lady Hillary Clinton was gearing up her campaign to become the next New York Junior US Senator in the Hamptons and needed someone that can help organize and get volunteer drivers for their motorcade. Eventually, I got a few Democratic party volunteers to help drive. We rented a few vans and headed to the Hamptons for a weekend with President Clinton, the First Lady, and their daughter, Chelsea.

Getting to the Hamptons from New York City took about two hours with heavy traffic. Each day, we received instructions from the White House staff on how to facilitate the day. The Secret Service would have me and my volunteers, ten drivers to be exact, report to a secured beach staging area so that our vehicles could be checked for bombs and any weapons that could hurt the President. We would then proceed to where President Clinton, and the First Lady were staying, they were guests of Steven Spielberg at his lavish and awesome mansion. For two days we had what appeared to be a sixty-car motorcade and visited some beautiful homes owned by the rich and famous. It was actually a cool experience. I had all the celebrities in my vehicle, like Wyclef Jean and his wife; I had some of the top senators in the van with me. I was the second vehicle behind the Presidential Limo, which was called "The Beast."

At the end of the assignment, they took us on the tarmac because the President and First Lady wanted to thank us for volunteering to help out. I was able to get a picture of me standing with Hillary Clinton. That experience made me like her. From that point on she definitely had my vote.

Life After the Councilwoman
At some point, about a few weeks after I resigned, the Councilwoman asked me to come back to work for her. I was offered a $10,000 salary increase. I did in fact go back for a few months then an opportunity presented itself as I was always looking for growth. So, I once again put in my resignation and was hired to work for the New York State Senate Democratic Minority Caucus. Working for the Senate I was now able to learn about the state level of politics and service to constituents, in addition I was assigned to the Reapportionment Task Force. See, The U.S. Constitution requires that congressional and state legislative district

boundaries be redrawn every ten years, reflecting population shifts detected by the Federal census. This process, referred to as "redistricting," is undertaken by the state Legislature. In New York State, the Legislative Task Force on Demographic Research and Reapportionment analyzes the Census Bureau population figures used in the redistricting plan. Some heavy stuff right? Well I was hired to be the State Director for African American outreach, what really grabbed me is that it was paying $20,000 more than the City council salary, so I was all in.

9/11

September eleventh is a day that no New Yorker will ever forget. I remember exactly where I was when the towers were hit. I was managing a campaign field operation and I had just finished dropping off all my election day poll site workers at the different polling sites throughout Brooklyn. After I dropped the last worker off, I went to put gas in my car as I was planning to go into the city to my office for a brief moment to do some paperwork when I noticed the world was coming to an end. Well, it seemed that way. All I saw was a lot of pandemonium happening around me in the street. People were freaking out, the street started clogging up with traffic. It was getting ridiculous! All of a sudden, I saw people running away from the city. I looked up to see this large plume of smoke hovering over the sky and was like, *damn there is a really big fire somewhere.* My phone started ringing and that's when I found out that we were under attack. I started calling all my kids to find out where they were and also my brothers so that we could all meet up and devise a plan to gather up the family to insure everyone was safe. It got to a point where we were ready to break out the bikes because traffic was at a standstill. Fortunately, everyone was safe, but we couldn't reach my step mother who had been through this before. I couldn't shake the thought that this reminded me of a TV show I saw where some kids on a high school football team wound up saving their small town from an invasion by Russia and Cuba, it was so surreal. Sorry back to my stepmother, she survived the 1993 bombing of the World Trade Center and yet here it was that she had to endure this madness all over again. It would be hours before we would find out that she was forced to evacuate the city on a boat. She wound up in Staten Island as a guest of some New Yorkers who opened their home up to her that she didn't even know for a few days. THAT'S THE NEW YORK I KNOW AND LOVE! She actually told us that she witnessed and heard the bodies falling from the towers and that the sound of the bodies hitting the ground was horrific.

We were able to find everyone in the family and they were all safe. My Aunt Brenda, who worked for Immigration, had to walk over the bridge to get out of the City and found her way to our apartment where she would stay overnight as the trains and everything were not running, plus she had to wash that soot off of her immediately. I reflected on the fact that if I had gone to the City, I too would've been caught out there as my job was right where World Trade Center building number seven collapsed. My car would've been parked precisely in a place where it would have been demolished. I dodged a huge bullet and began the process to get back to some form of normality. But I realized that this could've been more catastrophic, and I didn't get to do some more of the things I wanted. I needed to harness the information and skills I learned in this political game so that I could help more people. So, what do I do next?

Run Tony, Run

I had expressed an interest in running for office shortly after 911. I had no clue that it would ruffle some feathers. I just knew that I was going to run for this District leadership position, but the higher-ups of the Kings County Democratic party had other plans. One day the executive director came to my desk and asked, "You like your job?"

To which I replied, "What does that mean?" But I knew exactly what that meant when he asked. It meant that they were protecting the person that I was thinking about running against. At the moment, that's when I realized politics is not about the people. It's about folks covering for each other that basically aren't doing a damn thing for the community. I recognized that our elected officials, except for the Councilmember and Congressman I worked for, were also subjected to fail their constituents due to greed and self-aggrandizement.

But despite being told not to run, I said I was going to anyway. Who the hell are they to deny me my democratic right? Although I didn't run for district leader, I flirted with the idea that I was going to run against Senator Velmanette Montgomery just to give her a heart attack as a bit of payback when she didn't help me and my family back in 1983.

How the hell was she a senator and was clueless as to what to do to help her community? Scenarios like that are what encouraged me to run even though I was told not to.

Chapter Three

A Taste of Politics

The first political run I put my energy into was back in 2003. I ran against councilman James Davis, who for the most part had pissed me off. At the time I had to spend some time working with the Democratic party. I was responsible for putting up posters right after 9/11. You know, to try and encourage everybody to stay positive, not to let the terrorists win. That was kind of like the theme of the stuff that they posted. We wanted our country to be unified.

Now, on this particular day, I spent a good three or four hours out in the community putting up these posters on poles, only to find out that the work I'd done was in vain. When I thought I was finished I went back to look at what I did. You know, to pat myself on the back for the work I'd just put in for the purpose of unity. I also wanted the people I worked for to see what I'd done. When I went back to take some pictures, I didn't see any of the posters I'd put up. I thought I was going crazy. But I wasn't. All the posters were taken down. I can't front. I was pissed! I wanted to know who would be so trifling and come behind me to remove some posters that basically called for New Yorkers to unify. It wouldn't be long before I found the culprit.

The following morning at a subway station near my house, I ran across Councilman James E. Davis. He was out campaigning. Now, I heard murmurs that he may have been responsible for taking my posters down. So, when I saw him, I felt some kind of way. I wanted to know if he was indeed the person responsible, so I straight up asked. I took him by surprise when I approached him because he really didn't know who I was. I let him know that I was the person who put up the posters for the Democratic party and he smirked. He made it known to me that he was the one who removed the posters personally.

That pissed me off.

Here I am, trying to serve my community and encourage them to vote and this guy is sabotaging my work because he has a problem with the Democratic party. I let him know what he'd done was disrespectful. Apparently, he didn't like my tone because he challenged me. And I challenged him back. I told him I was going to take his seat by running against him in the upcoming election. But that didn't faze him. At the time, he didn't see me as a threat. And honestly, I only said it to piss him off. I really didn't have time to play politics. I was busy running my own businesses and raising my boys. It was my disgust for his arrogance and cockiness that triggered me to actually follow through.

After a few days and all my bravado passed, it dawned on me that I needed to get my ass in gear if I was going to be a formidable opponent to this very popular and outspoken, flashy guy. Truthfully, I never thought I would be able to win, but I damn sure wanted him to sweat a little bit. Somebody needed to knock him down a peg or two and I didn't mind being the one to do it. I spoke with a number of people that encouraged me to run as they knew I had worked previously for some elected officials and had the experience to serve. FYI... it is very easy to get a battery put in your back by folks, the real question is will they be there to help you out. I learned the hard way (keep reading).

I wasn't quite sure about how I was going to make this happen, but I was determined to figure it out. There was another young lady who considered running against James but figured that she couldn't beat him for whatever reason unknown to me and decided not to run. Knowing that he was running unopposed made me really want to move forward with being in this race. The one thing that I had on my side was that the

Democratic party didn't like him. It was no secret that the Kings County Democratic Party Boss/Assemblyman Clarence Norman and his minions did not care for James at all. So, I concluded that I needed to get their support somehow to actually win this thing. My thought was, with their support and all the resources they have at their beck and call, such an endorsement could make me more of a viable candidate.

Grind Time

So, now it was time to get on the grind and truth be told my work was cut out for me. Luckily, I had a little experience in this arena, so I already knew what needed to be done. The first thing I needed to do was pull a campaign team together ASAP. The next thing I needed was to raise money to be competitive. Money was and always is the root of all corruption in politics or should I say "politrics," and I really wanted no parts of this process. I didn't want to bring any foolishness or scam artists around me. Instead of using other people's money, I wanted to use my own. I actually used money I saved to get things started but had to follow campaign finance laws. Laws that were truly designed to help incumbents and not the challengers of these overly entitled buffoons.

When the Democratic party heard that I was serious about running, they welcomed the challenge. Word had it that some friends in my network started buzzing about helping me to run and it got back to the Democratic party through their network. I guess they saw my candidacy as an opportunity to eliminate the guy they considered to be an enemy. They eventually came to me and said they would like to support me. So, me getting this much needed support was a no brainer, I excitedly said, "Yes, let's go for it!"

Because of the fact that I worked previously for elected officials in the borough, I had access to all of their connections. Any fear that I had about running was reduced once I knew the largest Democratic party in the country was backing me. They would be sure to help me with whatever was needed to win this campaign, but fundraising was on me. That was cool. I knew I could and would handle that or so I thought, remember the battery in the back comment I made earlier?

While I was on cloud nine, I'm sure James wasn't too happy to hear this. He eventually learned who I was after all his boastful rants. He found out that I was a very popular party promoter who had at one point had his own video magazine TV show for several years and was a local radio show host and producer. I'm sure he may have just realized I could become a viable threat that he had to acknowledge and couldn't ignore. Yea...Tony Herbert could potentially snatch his seat!

The pressure was on and I felt every bit of it. I had a lot of people expecting me to take James' spot. And frankly I was expecting to do just that as well. So, I stepped up my game and got my team together. I made sure we were on point and in position to be seen as a threat to James and his campaign. We didn't play dirty, though. Just used facts to be seen and heard in the community. Fundraising became the priority as did getting on the ballot, which was not a very easy thing to do. This was and always has been a challenge with new candidates attempting to run against seasoned candidates who were incumbents. Getting donations from grass roots folk is like pulling teeth, even family was hard to pitch and for the life of me I just didn't understand why. I hated asking for donations, it felt like begging and I wasn't good at it at all. At any rate, the race was on and I had to suck it up and beg for support. All the support I could potentially receive made it a surreal moment.

Running my first campaign will always be a great memory. The highs, the lows, the wins, the losses - all of it contributed to me being the man I am today. But I have to say, one of the most memorable moments of the campaign was when I was presented to the politically powerful First Baptist Church of Crown Heights congregation as their candidate for City Council. I had my sons with me. So, you know I had to make sure we were suited! It was a packed house with a bunch of Judges and other elected officials. I was introduced in front of a lot of power brokers from the community. Everybody stood up to acknowledge me; that's when everything shifted for me. It was in that very moment that I felt I was in a real campaign. I got a sense of acceptance that I would finally be in a position to really help people, unlike when that senator couldn't or wouldn't help me and my family.

So, yeah, I hit the street to begin petitioning to get on the ballot and rallying support from the people who were associated with the party. I knocked on doors, talked to people at the train stations, stood outside of supermarkets to gather signatures - you name it, we did it. It was during this phase that I noticed I was truly a threat to James. This is where the race between him and I got more and more interesting. I'd learned that he was threatening to cut funding and/or close his doors to anyone that supported me. People would tell me that he would go on and on with his, "I am the best" rants whenever my name was mentioned. A female friend even told me that he was told, "'Well, you got some competition now James because you aren't the only one that's handsome, Tony Herbert looks just as good.' Boy, oh boy did he get hot!" she said. Hilarious! It must have been some truth to what she was saying because he would always poke out his chest whenever I would show up at the same community events he was at. I had dude shook!

I recall being at a street fair in Prospect Heights on Flatbush Avenue one Saturday; I ran into James and we exchanged slight pleasantries, but if anyone was looking, they could see that we really weren't cool with each other. We were clearly only speaking for obvious reasons. We didn't want to allude to any tension between us, but oh it was there. I had two of my three sons with me, Anthony was seven and Antone was five at the time. I had my nephew, Lil' Nate, as well who was around seven. I remember that I bought them some silly string to play with. Then I got a crazy idea to get under James' skin. So, I put the kids up to spraying James with the silly stuff just to irk him....and wow did it work! So, much so that James came over and played it off by throwing a football type shoulder block into my chest that winded me slightly. Truthfully, dude's upper body was tight, and I felt that impact. I took it, and then later on thought that I should've laid down on the ground and screamed he had just assaulted me. Ha! But I had the kids with me and didn't want to put them through that trauma. However, it would've been a really good press hit. I can see the headline now, "Councilman Assaults Political Rival"... hilarious! Now that would've made some serious noise. We had a number of similar interactions during the campaign. Most verbally, though. Ironically, I didn't dislike James. It was the self-proclaimed superman he tried to portray himself to be that I had a problem with, but I respected him.

S*** Got Real

I'll never forget the dreadful day that impacted me and my position in the campaign in a major way. I play it over and over in my head all the time. It was July 23rd, 2003. At five a.m. that morning my phone rang. To this day I get terribly concerned when I get calls at that time. It usually isn't a call that isn't absent of some kind of tragic news. The caller didn't have any tragic news; however, it was only the beginning of a tragedy I didn't see coming.

The unexpected call was from Aaron Othneil Askew, another candidate for the council seat. He wasn't as well known in the community but bragged a lot about his finances and how he could win the race. Problem was he couldn't stand a chance at winning with me in the race. He was calling to get me to back out of the race so that he can run against James in the Primary. I politely blew him off and ignored his ranting. It was five a.m. and my brain wasn't up yet. Somewhere in between his ranting, he asked me to meet him at Tom's, one of the most popular diners in the community around eight a.m. I declined his invite because I had too many meetings lined up that day. And plus he was acting kind of weird, talking crazy and I wasn't about to entertain him. He even had the audacity to ask me if I was recording our call. Before I could tell him hell no, he hung up, and called me right back. Then he asked me if I was willing to die for the council seat like he was. I didn't even bother answering that dumb question. I looked at the phone and just shook my head. Strangely I didn't think two ways about the question and chalked it up to just more of his rambling antics. He stated, "Tony, you are a good guy," before wishing me good luck. And just like that the conversation was over.

I let the conversation with Askew go in one ear and out of the other so I could get my day started. Later that morning, I had to report my campaign activity to the Pastor who got me the Party's support. We were to meet at one of the senior centers he managed. When I arrived, he kindly let me know that he was slightly perturbed with me because I didn't have an actual glowing fundraising report. He did however say something that has stayed with me until this day. He said, "You gotta take this thing seriously. People die in this game."

I said, "Yes, sir," and told him I would step up my efforts.

My team and I left so I could get ready for our next meeting. I was scheduled to meet with an attorney friend who was going to help prep me for a good government organization endorsement interview for later that afternoon. And guess where we planned to meet?

At a breakfast diner right around the corner from James' City Council district office! I thought about the conversation that I had earlier with Askew and just brushed it off again.

It was around 11:45 a.m. or so that we wrapped up and my cell phone started going off. I ignored the first few calls but then my cell kept blaring. I answered the call and was shocked by the words that left this community leader's lips. It was Darnell Canada from Fort Greene and he called to say that someone had just been shot inside City Hall, a council person is involved and there are a whole bunch of cops swarming on the building. I paused for a minute and my first thought was, only two council members carry guns because they were former law enforcement officers, that would be James Davis and Hiram Montserrat. My random thought was that James went and shot someone protecting his colleagues. So, damn! Now he would be considered a hero and more difficult to beat in the election.

Great!

Wanting to hear more about what has just happened I jumped in the car to turn on the radio to 1010 Wins as I made my way home. About seven minutes or so later, I made it home and rushed upstairs to turn the TV on. I wanted to see if the news I'd heard over the phone would be plastered all over the airwaves. Within minutes of arriving home my doorbell started ringing feverishly. I answered the bell. It was some guy that said he was sent from One Police Plaza to check on me as per the Chief of Dept/Chief Esposito whom I considered a friend. So, I buzzed him in thinking that was nice of the Chief in lieu of what had just happened at City Hall to check to make sure I was safe. I'd soon find out that was not the real reason for his visit.

The Plot Thickens

The Detective knocked on my door after navigating the four flights he had to climb to get to my apartment. Given he was a little overweight, it looked like he had a hard time, if you know what I mean! As he is catching his breath, he introduced himself again as a homicide detective from One Police Plaza. I let him in and we both walked back to my living room where I had the TV on. He was sweating a bit. I tried not to embarrass him by staring and turn my attention to the TV. At that point, the cameras caught the EMT medics bringing out two gurneys. The first looked to have Councilman Davis on it and they were pumping his chest profusely.

Then my bell rings several more times like back to back so I buzzed it to let whomever in. Before I knew it, I had damn near fifty Police officers in my apartment. A few of the Community Affairs officers I knew asked me to step into another room and asked what I had said to the homicide detective. I responded, "What should I have said? I said nothing!" They were like, "good." Then my phone rang, and it was my Pastor, Rev H. Devore Chapman, calling to see if I was okay. Next, Congressman Town's attorney called to ask the same thing and told me if I needed him to give him a call. I never spoke to dude before so I was quite surprised that he called, plus I couldn't afford him even if I did need him!

By now I was all sorts of confused. Why was everyone asking if I was okay? I'm not the one who was shot. Then I got the craziest call. Political reporter Errol Louis called and asked why did I do it? Did I do it?

At that moment it all became clear. The detective, then the community affairs officers and cops, the calls from the attorney, my pastor then bang... Errol Louis!

Wait, was I a suspect in the shooting of Councilman Davis?

Chapter Four

Guilty or Nah?

It was being reported by some eyewitnesses that James was shot by his political opponent, however no one knew of Aaron Othniel Askew. They did however know that I was running against James. I was told that the eyewitness said, "It was that bald head guy with glasses, and he ran down in the subway." Can you believe that these fools shut the subway system down to search for me?

Okay, so let's make this make sense. If I had indeed shot James and escaped in the subway system, I would've had to wait on the train and New York was notorious for not running on time, take an express train out of Manhattan toward Brooklyn, go about seven stops, transfer to a local train and go about four more stops, then walk about five blocks to get home after allegedly shooting someone and not act suspiciously. All in time to open my door for a homicide detective to watch me twenty minutes after the shooting. Hmmmm! Does that make sense?

The day of the shooting, I had on a crisp white button-down shirt. It wasn't wrinkled or soiled from sweat. I mean, a man that just shot someone and had ran away from the scene, to Brooklyn, they would certainly be drenched in sweat, right?

With fifty police officers in my apartment and a whole SWAT team who closed off the streets outside my apartment building, it was evident I was considered a suspect for a brief moment. Thankfully, they did their investigation at City Hall thoroughly and found I totally had nothing to do with the shooting of Councilman James Davis.

The real suspect, Aaron Othniel Askew, the "other candidate" was shot inside City Hall's Chamber after an officer who was on duty protecting the Speaker of the City Council shot him.

The cops were with me for at least an hour and I am sure they all concluded that I had nothing to do with all that had taken place at City Hall. I fielded more calls from family and friends while staying glued to the news reports of what happened. Then James was pronounced dead at the hospital. It was all kind of frantic at City Hall I was told. Askew went to City Hall with James in his car, I mean hell, he could've killed James then. By him going to City Hall to commit this assassination, Askew was trying to make a statement, but we would've never had known what that was because he too was killed

It was James's bravado I believe that allowed Askew to get the drop on him when he walked that dude around that magnetometer. James waived him past the one piece of equipment that may have very well saved his life. But why? He didn't need to play up to Askew, because there was no way Askew was going to beat James for the seat. I had a better chance than Askew to get close to beating him at least.

So, after all the Cops left my apartment once getting the word from City Hall that the investigation had concluded and I was no longer a suspect, I went outside only to witness my neighbors whispering. There was a single police van still sitting in front of my building. I'm guessing they were there in the event that I was guilty, and they could haul my ass off to jail, naturally I am being sarcastic.

I got a chance to talk to a few neighbors and they explained to me what they saw outside. I was like wow; they sent an army for me, huh?

After the Dust Cleared
I had heard that there was going to be an impromptu memorial at Brown Memorial Baptist Church for Councilman Davis and

decided I wanted to go and show support. I was greeted with a very dark and seedy eye-piercing stare from Councilman Davis' brother Geoffrey Davis. Geoffrey for whatever reason believed I had something to do with his brother's murder; despite the fact that the police had already killed the man responsible for James' death.

I ignored Geoffrey and stayed at the church for a while. While I made my rounds and talked with a few community folks, my phone started ringing off the hook yet again, it was news reporters who wanted to talk with me about the shooting. I was confused because I didn't have anything to do with that, so I wasn't sure why they were calling me. Wouldn't take long for me to figure out why.

It had gotten out that Askew called me that morning and the news was going to print a story written by Errol Louis that, "The shooter may have had a double homicide on his mind," based on some taped phone recordings the police found in his home. They determined that Askew wanted to kill me as well, so that's why he called me that morning to meet up.

That must have been the recordings he made at which time he accused me of recording him. I must admit that dude was acting kind of irrational, but again it was early in the morning and I wasn't quite awake yet, so I blew it off.

Chapter Five

All Bets Are Off

As the city mourned the death of the only elected official to ever be killed in New York City Hall , the reality that we still had an election that had to take place was real, so I got right back to business. I had my team in place, my campaign finance paperwork prepared, I was ready to hit the pavement running. However, my calls to all those who said they were supporting me weren't being returned. I even called the powerful Pastor and was disappointed with what he had said to me. He told me that things had changed and that there was no way I would beat James' mother for the seat.

Huh? When was it determined I would be running against a seventy-nine-year-old woman? I had no clue that a decision was made to allow James' mother to run in place of him. And he said because the community had so much compassion for the family in their time of bereavement, that there was no way I'd beat his mother. He basically told me they no longer had any interest in supporting me for the seat. It had become too much of a controversy and frankly they wanted no parts, especially with his mother being the candidate. Turns out it was a ceremonial gesture at best because it only lasted for a few days. As James' brother Geoffrey proclaimed he was the rightful heir.

See, each candidate had to pick a "committee to elect" should anything happen to them like death or they moved out of the state. So, James' committee selected his brother Geoffrey.

Great.

Now, let's be clear - Geoffrey Davis was no James Davis, but he was in a better position to get the Democratic nod now more so than ever. However, I was a bump in the road and albeit we didn't have any beef that I knew of, rest assured he wasn't happy that I was blocking his chances. At some point, as luck would have it, Geoffrey began to implode. The media pounced on him with a vengeance. The day James died, Geoffrey all but accused the media of his death. So, he opened up a can of whoop ass and they began digging up all kinds of stories from his past about alleged domestic violence, child support issues, and how he needed anger management because he allegedly burned up his girlfriend's car and tried to drag her out of a meeting. I didn't need to go after him and throw him under the bus, he was sabotaging himself. Giving all this drama the Democratic party fell back from supporting him too. That made me feel a little better. However I didn't take it personal for them to not support me after this move. They wanted a squeaky-clean, controversy-free candidate and that clearly wasn't Geoffrey. Nor did they want someone they couldn't control, hence why I feel they pulled back from supporting me. After all, that was their problem with James.

Now, I wasn't shocked that things got a little crazy after James' death. What I didn't expect to happen was for things to get as dirty as they had. But oh, yes they did indeed!

You see, I found out a few days before James died, that he filed to challenge my petitions and that challenge was kept in play by Geoffrey. This meant that any petition I filed to get on the ballot would be challenged in court to knock me off the ballot. This is what is called Ballot Bumping. Ballot Bumping is a legal, but immoral, tool most politicians use to get rid of their challengers, and James was scared enough to pull this stunt on me. But I wasn't having any of that. I declared I was going to fight for my spot. They were going to have a tough time bumping me off the ballot!

I felt even more validated when I received some unexpected support along the way by this attorney who I will call Mr. Dan. Mr. Dan came out of the blue and offered to assist me in my efforts to get on the ballot for free. I was overwhelmed with the amount of support I was getting, so one more person who knew how to navigate the balloting process was awesome. I welcomed him with open arms. After all, he applauded my efforts in the community and wanted to help. I told him about the fiasco with Ballot Bumping and he assured me I would be good to go when the time came for me to file my papers. I was beyond grateful when he took the lead in preparing my paperwork for court. I was new to all of this, so his help was much appreciated.

When I realized their plan of attack on me, I came up with my own plan of attack on them. I made a few calls and got a judge to sign a subpoena to keep the Board of Elections open the weekend before my court appearance. I made this request so that I along with a host of volunteers, could check and verify the voter registrations of those signatures that were being challenged against the Board of Elections computers. I had to identify and confirm those good signatures were good that James challenged and said weren't valid. For two days, my volunteers helped me identify 177 signatures that were just that - valid! The painstaking process paid off and that was more than I needed to qualify and get on the ballot. Ya boy was hopefully back in the game! I had the proof that would show the Board of Elections that I did everything the right way. I was legit and deserved that spot on that ballot. Mr. Dan escorted me to where I needed to go in the Supreme Court building, so that I could file my papers for the hearing. I thought, *that's it! Papers filed. I am now gonna get my day in court...* or was I?

It was now Monday morning and I was to appear before a Democratic politically appointed judge by the Kings County Democrats, who was totally controlled by the party. All weekend long I prepared for this moment. I was ready to get it over with so I could get back to campaigning. I remember walking into the courtroom feeling vindicated. I wasn't guilty of doing anything wrong, I even had proof that I did the right thing. Got Mr. Dan on my side. All was well over here. Finally, our case was called. I sat up and waited for the session to get started. The gavel sounded and my opponent's attorney jolted right out the gate like a thoroughbred seeking to win the triple crown. He stated to the judge that my petition to be heard by the court was not valid, as it suffered a "Fatal Flaw." In his loud tone of excitement, you would have thought he just found Jimmy Hoffer the way he spoke.

Fatal Flaw? What did that even mean? I was confused as all hell at that point and got more fed up with the whole deal. Here was yet another issue with this damn campaign. It appeared that my petition that Mr. Dan filed for me did not get stamped on its first page, thus rendering me to be unable to be heard in court, thus creating the Fatal Flaw!

Now I'm even more confused. If Mr. Dan knew that I couldn't be heard without that stamp, why didn't he make sure that everything was done right? Why didn't the clerk who had the responsibility of stamping my paperwork notice he didn't complete his job? All of a sudden I got a weird feeling in my gut. I thought to myself, *wait, Mr. Dan knew he was supposed to have known what he was doing?* Then felt like I had just gotten played. The clerk at the court didn't stamp the first page on purpose! He was hired by the court as an appointee from the Democratic party so naturally they had him in on sabotaging my papers. I thought about how eager Mr. Dan was to help me, and for free, *how did I not see this coming?* I never met the man, he just appeared out of thin air to help me. I should have known something was up. It was then that the political reporter from channel four who was seated behind me in the courtroom whispered in my ear that they were railroading me. She personally saw the judge getting hand signals from the Executive Director of the Democratic Party taking his cues from him from the back of the room.

At that point in my mind I felt defeated, I sat back in my seat and basically threw my hands up. I just witnessed the very party I pledged my allegiance to since the age of eighteen steal my opportunity to officially be effective for my community.

But why?

The Fix Is In!
After finding out from some political insiders that I was indeed being railroaded, I became distraught. Then I got upset. I couldn't help but think about all of the turmoil, the work, the time, the personal and financial sacrifice I put into this campaign only to have it ripped right from my fingertips. I didn't understand why the Democrats would put all that time into pretending to support me. They weren't supporting Geoffrey, so why sabotage me? Hmmm... I did say sabotage right? Yep. It all

became very clear as to what had just happened...

So, word had it that the darling of the Democratic Party TJ found a way to get on the ballot via the Working Families Party. It seems that a deal was cut between them and the Democratic Party Bosses to support her as the candidate for the seat since they had realized Geoffrey was no longer an option and that I wouldn't be controlled. Truthfully, if these shenanigans didn't come into play, I would've beat Geoffrey and became the Democratic nominee for the Thirty-Fifth Councilmanic District. But this late entry candidate had other plans. I also found out that Mr. Dan just happened to be the treasurer for TJ's campaign which gives every impression that he was sent to intentionally sabotage my petition filing.

Case Closed, Democracy Denied

As I walked down that long hallway in the court building to the elevators alone after being knocked off the ballot my heart was hurting. The Democratic Party decided they wanted someone they can control in that seat, I was replaced. Feeling defeated and drained given all those days and nights out on the campaign trail, being disrespected because I was a so-called politician, chastised and on occasion called out my name because those before me didn't do a damn thing when they were in office. Yeah what was it all for, what do I have to show for the time away from my kids and family by just wanting to help others?

As I exited the court building, it seemed eerily quiet, but a lot of folks were going about their business as usual. Yet I couldn't help but feel alone, there were a couple of news reporters from the New York Times and Spectrum News NY1 who were waiting to get an interview with me about what had just happened. I told them, "I was just robbed of my constitutional right to run for office by the very people who were supposed to uphold my democracy." I went on to say that..."The democratic party just walked away from me to do what was politically expedient for their greed and need to control elections in our community while unfairly disenfranchising me as a tax paying citizen of our city, thus creating a further sense of distrust of politics."

Wait - It Ain't Over
Just as I completed the interviews on the steps of the court building, a tall white guy, who looks a little like the nutty Professor in the Back To

The Future movies named Robert, pulled me aside and asked if "I had considered running on another party line as well to stay in the race?"

My first reaction was to respond with no, but then I realized that I could run on a major party line and still be considered a contender, so I asked him how and what it is I have to do?"

He said, "The Republican party could be considered, although they have a candidate already, we can work to get you a Wilson Pakula."

To which I replied, "What the hell is that?" He explained that a Wilson Pakula is an authorization given by a political party to a candidate for public office in the State of New York that allows the candidate not registered with that party to run as its candidate in a given election.

I was like let's do it! This was an opportunity I felt which will allow me to still run and be a contender for the council seat. However, running as a republican was an issue in a heavily democratic city. With no visions of grandeur, I knew this a huge uphill battle and my chances of winning were very dismal, but at least I could keep the concerns and issues of the community in the debate and the conversation to be had as these career politicians spew their rhetoric.

Chapter Six

So, Now What?

Leaving that courtroom feeling defeated, as though all that campaigning was for not didn't sit well with me! All the late nights at community meetings, running around the district meeting with folks trying to convince them that I could make a difference if they would only cast their vote for me, and here it is now a Wilson Pakula could keep me in the game.

I ran into a lot of potential supporters and a whole lot of haters as well who didn't even know me! I kept thinking, I just couldn't let things end like this because I had too much to offer and a lot of great ideas on how to better service the constituents that reside in the very community I was born, raised, educated, and worked in.

After a few meetings with the Republican leadership and a unanimous vote, they agreed to give me their line. I do believe there was one white guy from Park slope that was a hater and voted against me but that didn't matter, all the other District leaders did.

But man, I wanted to be in the race so badly after all that had transpired, and I needed to prove that I wasn't a quitter and that we needed a candidate that wasn't bought and sold by the establishment. The Republican ballot line would allow me to continue as a serious candidate and yeah, I got it.

Interestingly, they moved heaven and earth for me to get it. It was a really crazy situation, like why did they choose to go through such changes to accommodate me? I mean they literally pushed the candidate Frank V out of the country so that I could get on their ballot line.

However, I did understand why... because my candidacy could possibly attract other minorities (Black folk) to want to run on the Republican line in the future and that would give their party a serious boost. They get a little something and I get a little something. Hell that's how things go down in politics all the time! The beauty is that I did not have to run on a typical ideological Republican platform which made things even better for me.

It's Election Day and the Foolery Began
So, I got my campaign team and supporters geared up and the workers were assigned to man their polling sites throughout the district. What I learned later on that day was that the Democratic party along with the Working Family Party which was the line my opponent

was on, sent out their workers to solicit my campaign workers to throw my literature away and they would pay them, some were even paid and sent home it was alleged.

What ever happened to democracy? The Democratic party became immorally inept and in violation of their own mission statement. Were they that scared that I could possibly beat them by being in the race on the Republican line?

You know the saying politics makes for strange bedfellows is real and will turn those who claim to be your friend against you. Case in point, when I was hired by Congressman Towns back in 1999, I was assigned to be his liaison in the Fort Greene/Clinton Hill area of his district. Since I was born in Cumberland Hospital right there in the heart of Fort Greene, it made it easier for me to interact with the residents as they saw me as a neighbor. So, I immediately began to seek out who the community leaders were and poured a lot of energy into them to reel them in so as to support the Congressman for his re-election bid, as he had lost some ground due to what was being perceived as a broken promise to bring jobs into the community from the big Marriott hotel development deal in addition to the fact that there was a potential candidate who was making noise and challenging my boss, I had to nip all that in the bud.

The Fort Greene area is heavy with Public Housing projects and where I decided to go to begin building a strong base for the boss. I targeted building a relationship with one of the guys in the hood named DC who was doing a lot of community outreach programs out of his pocket and had a lot of blood credibility, he was a former drug dealer who had got into the construction business by scouting out jobs for young residents of the projects who wanted to work, they called what he was doing... "Shaping." I believed we had built a really strong friendship and we did a lot of good things for the community together over a course of time and even hung out leisurely.

You see, DC had just finished seven years in federal prison for allegedly threatening a construction supervisor, and in my efforts to help point him in the right direction, we became friends or so I thought and I introduced him to the world of politics, we hung out at family events, I even gave him what he needed to become more respected in the hood, I gave him political credibility. Now remember I said politics makes for strange bedfellows. Well DC made things messy when he flipped on me for the almighty dollar. I introduced him to my opponent when she first came into the community. Big mistake!

My political opponent on the Working Family Party line moved in to pull his support away from me by telling him he could get access to lucrative developers and contracts that she could introduce him to, and he could make a lot of money with them if he rolled with her and supported her candidacy. So, that's what he did, and even tried to dirty my name.

I felt totally betrayed but it was a learning curve and is the main reason why I don't get close to or even trust people in politics, even up until today. Ironically after a few years we started talking again but I just couldn't trust him, so I kept him at an arm's distance. He had since past away due to complications of AIDS messing around having unprotected sex with a lot of women and guess who raised the money and organized his funeral… yep me!

But it was DC who flipped the workers on my campaign in his effort to support my opponent which caused me to lose much support at the polling sites. Damn!

So, I lost the election and was left with a lot of campaign debt. I was fined for some accounting errors by campaign finance and sued personally by the guy we rented campaign space from. Yep that's all I had to show for my first attempt to run for office and still paying for that election in 2020. My campaign team managers were not experienced campaign managers and made mistakes, but I appreciated their effort.

Chapter Seven

Politics Chose Me

If someone would have told the eighteen-year-old me that one day I would run for city councilman, be a part of a high-profile murder plot, get thrown under the bus during my campaign, meet three Presidents of this country, or stand on the front lines of injustice to help defend my community I would have laughed!

While I didn't expect to have any of the experiences that I did, I appreciate each of them. Every experience, situation, and circumstance I encountered over the years made me who I am today. A husband, father, leader, and voice for the people. The people who don't have the voice to get the attention their problems deserve; those are the people who I speak for. And everything I've been through has given me the courage to be that voice.

I'll tell you one thing, I certainly didn't choose this path. This path was chosen for me. I was chosen to be the vessel that encourages people to fight for their rights. I was selected to boldly intercede between my community and city officials. I'm one of the people who stands on the front line - and while it's my passion, it's not easy. One of the biggest challenges is getting push back from your own and a lack of support. Look, It's a lot of work to do but not many people have the thick skin or tenacity to get it done. Our communities need more people like me, hell I need more people like me as the struggle is real. We have to push past the infighting, and crabs in the barrel mentality, we can only advance if we work together. There is no "I" in team. There's power in numbers. When we all come together for the greater good, amazing things can happen.

So, what is it I want you to walk away with from reading my book?

Simple: I want to remind you that you have the power and the politicians are supposed to work for you it's not the other way around.

Albeit we may come from different upbringings, different religions, different beliefs, communities, and/or we may have been raised under different socio-economic situations, our common denominator is that we want to be respected and treated as the decent human beings that we are. We want the people that we put in office to lead us to do just that. The only way we can do this is by coming together and making our voices heard. How? We do that by VOTING!

I know many of you believe that your vote doesn't count or matter, oh but it does! It can be proven to you if you go out and vote. One of the reasons change isn't happening is because people give up their right to vote. And I get it, politicians don't always keep their word so you're reluctant and don't trust them. That's where people like me come in, to hold them accountable. However, people like me can't do what needs to be done if the community doesn't support the full movement. This means joining us on the front line, getting to know the officials in your community, showing up, and VOTING. You matter and your VOTE has power. If you want those potholes on your street fixed - **VOTE**. Want the crime to subside in your neighborhood? **VOTE**. Does your neighborhood need a community center for the kids? **VOTE**. The only way for things to get better in our communities is to **VOTE** for the RIGHT person to make these things happen.

Look, we all want to live in safe communities free of any form of violence, a city where elected officials do their job honorably as well as to ensure that the taxes we pay to this government is working for us. We also want our right to vote to be respected and not manipulated by self-serving politicians looking to secure seats for themselves or their friends that they aid in selling off our communities to the highest bidders. It's no secret that they often forget why they were elected in the first place... but we'll remind them that WE NEED THEM TO SERVE THE COMMUNITY WITH DIGNITY, PROFESSIONALISM AND RESPECT OF THEIR CONSTITUENTS!

That's the life I and many of you deserve. It's the life that I'm fighting on your behalf for. Our children should not have to worry about their tomorrow, nor should they fear a lack of political leadership that does not represent them or even afford them the same rights and privileges that we continue to seek and have always fought for. We stand on the shoulders of a great many people that came before us and shed their blood in order for us to do so. People are hungry for change. Voting will cure that hunger pain. So, go out and **VOTE!**

Know that local elections are just as important as national elections, so show up for those as well. Be sure to do your research about those who wish to represent you. Don't throw your vote away just because you know their name. Vote because you know the work that they do and have been doing. Ask them the questions that you feel you need to know. Take heed to their alliances and to those who they support to determine if they are aligned with who and what you are familiar with or believe. Most elected officials hire people due to political favor, sadly their staffers aren't really trained in doing social work or are familiar with social services, thus creating a disconnect with the community.

But do note, that if you go to any elected officials office they are obligated by their oath of office to help navigate you through whatever municipal situation you're faced with by plugging you into the correct governmental office and should team up with their colleagues in order to help guide you correctly before stating, "That you are in the wrong gov't office." If that elected official's office isn't holding your hand and going the extra yard to assist you, then that's a reflection on that person's lack of knowing and or understanding the job they were elected/ hired to do.

The most important nugget I want you to walk away with is to encourage young people to fight for a seat at the table. For far too often politicians talk about what our youth need but never talk to the youth or invite them to the table thus causing generational separation. These are the people we should be listening to because they're experiencing the results of our vote. Having a different perspective can help officials make better decisions.

To my people that live in Public Housing both here in NYC and throughout the country, you are a sleeping giant. With millions of residents and a large portion of voters living amongst you, you have the ability to change the dynamics of politics in your city overnight, if you only came out to vote. Residents of Public Housing being organized as a voting block is a serious threat and potential nightmare for a lot of do-nothing political and special interest groups who wish to keep you silent. If you're silent, their communities can continue to flourish and grow, while you face the highest rates of evictions, unsanitary and unsafe conditions in your development due to a lack of repairs, services, and resources along with a lack of respect for you as residents.

This can all change by getting to know your officials, putting in your demands, and voting.

I encourage you, no I implore you to go to all your community meetings be they the

Precinct Council, Community Board, Tenant Association, PTA meetings and/or your local block association meetings to get the info that will afford you to become more knowledgeable about what is going on in your community. Elected officials or aspiring candidates go to these meetings and share a lot of info about others who take interest in moving you out.

To my young people, please get involved and engaged with what is being decided on in your community. Too many conversations and meetings are being had about you and what others feel you need but you never get invited to the table, it's time you take control of the conversations and get your rightful seat to participate in these discussions and decisions being made about the very community you will inherit.

While I may not have dreamt about being a voice for the people when I was a kid, it's become a dream for me. Being able to impact my community with actions and not just words are important to me. I will continue to serve my community and be at the forefront of the movement and fighting for what's right! I believe that things will get better and I know this to be true because I will continue to stand up for what my community needs, and that's a fair and equal chance at living the American dream.

So, I will see you at the Polls and don't let anyone or any political party hold you or your Vote... hostage!

Meet Tony

Anthony L. Herbert, Sr., affectionately known to all as Tony, is a Community Leader who has a broad range of corporate, political, community and business leadership experience.

A Brooklyn native – born in Ft Greene and raised in Prospect Heights – Tony attended public grammar, middle school, and high school in the Fort Greene and Clinton Hill neighborhoods. His interest in community affairs began during his formative years while being raised in a single-parent household. Tony's mother, the sole breadwinner and a dedicated school aide for over 30 years in the NYC public school system before passing of Cancer in 1999, instilled in him core family values, a solid work ethic, and the desire to serve others.

In 1983, during Tony's early teenage years, the onset of gentrification caused Tony and his family to become homeless. They lived as squatters in an abandoned building in Prospect Heights. That experience was the foundation upon which Tony's commitment to community service was built. Today, Tony stands in the gap to provide a voice for those who can't speak for themselves.

Tony currently serves as the Community Relations Officer for The Ravenswood Generating Station in addition to President/CEO and Chairman of the Multi-Cultural Restaurant & NightLife Chamber of Commerce, Founder and President of the Advocates Without Borders Network. He is an executive committee member of the NAACP-NYCHA Branch Chapter; Executive Vice President of Youth Step USA; President of The National Action Network's NY Public Housing Chapter, member of the MW Prince Hall Grand Masonic Lodge of New York State -SOK#123; a member of Rehoboth Cathedral and a proud member of United Goodwill Temple Community Church.

Tony was employed as Special Assistant to former New York City Councilwoman Priscilla Wooten, Special Assistant to former Congressman Edolphus Towns, and Statewide Director of African American Affairs for the NY State Senate Minority Re-apportionment Task Force. He was also formerly employed as a Vocational/Educational Specialist for a Mentally Ill Homeless Women's Shelter in the East New York section of Brooklyn.

Through his position as Managing Director for the small business advocacy organization, the Diversity Business Alliance - Tony developed strong media relationships. He has been a featured guest, host and commentator on national and local radio/television news broadcasts including CNN, Radio One, TV One, The Tom Joyner Morning Show, Geraldo Rivera, Fox News, The Ernie Anastos Show, WBLS Open Line, Hot 97 with Lisa Evers, CBS, WABC, News 12, The John Gambling Show, and The Brooklyn Archdiocese News Network.

Tony frequently appears on the nightly news speaking out on issues such as New York City Housing, Gang & Gun Violence, Homelessness, Affordable Housing, Politics, Sex Trafficking, and Missing and Exploited Children.

Tony maintains relationships in the financial industry stemming from his past service as Senior Vice President of Government Relations and Small Business Development for Bridgepoint Capital and as a Business Banking Concierge for North Fork Bank.

Tony is newly married to Mrs. Leah Herbert.

He is also the father of four, and he currently resides in New York City.